Rhymes for the Times

Written by John O. Gray

Cover art by B. C. Fowler

ISBN 979-8-89309-158-8 (Paperback)
ISBN 979-8-89309-159-5 (Digital)

Covenant Books
11661 Hwy 707
Murrells Inlet, SC 29576
www.covenantbooks.com

Contents

Acknowledgments

Thanks to my dear sisters for their commitment to making this vision a reality: Wanda Roberts, Sara Jimenez, Patricia Holloway, Debra Chandler, Carol Banks, and Darlene Jones.

I also thank my eighth-grade English teacher, Patricia Jones, for encouraging me to continue writing down my thoughts.

Special thanks to my best friend and wife, Saundra. I'm truly experiencing Ecclesiastes 4:9–12 KJV: "Two are better than one; because they have a good reward for their labour." (Ecclesiastes 4:9-12 KJV)

Thank you for enhancing me, both naturally and spiritually (Proverbs 18:16).

To my sons, Ahmad and David Jordan, remain focused.

Preface

I was inspired to write these life lessons in rhyme not to criticize but with the sincere hope that the reader would confront their personal issues, trusting the Lord to bring healing, though it may be painful. For God desires truth in the inward parts. These scars are a reality. Too often, our families are portals through which these scars establish residence in our minds and manifest in our behavior.

> For as a man thinketh in his heart, so is he.
> (Proverbs 23:7)

In my youth, I became a victim of numerous scars passed down from previous generations, entangled in an environment of wounded family members and friends. I'm eternally grateful to my Lord Jesus for this creative gift He has given me to help free people from the inward scars inflicted upon the souls of God's people—scars that have grown and now dictate our behavior. May the peace that surpasses all understanding become your portion in Jesus's name.

Father Me

Fathers are the gas to the engine,
Negative rebuttal whenever his name is mentioned;
Family structure twisted and unstable
Some tasks, mamas aren't able

Fathers flood child-support court;
Society has made this a revolving sport
Meditating on the conditions in the land;
Certain knowledge and wisdom only comes from a man
There's an expected end, proper structure where purpose begins
Dissecting life's puzzle, they go about;
Minus a father, too often in doubt,
Young souls perish in the street,
Yearning for a father's love they seek

A place in the universe boys need to reach;
Lessons that only a father can teach;
The depths of my soul thirst to be free
The love from a father to water me
Tormented to find my role; at every turn, females are in control
Absolutely, I love Mama; with unmarried mothers comes much drama
Black families live with immeasurable grief
Fathers are the medicine that brings relief

Schoolin' My Sons

Son, you don't want a girl like Sally.
She bumps and grinds in a dirty alley.
Fabricated stories, she's from Callie.
You can hear Sally's head bangin' on the bedroom wall.
She's got more fingerprints than an NBA ball.
Sunday morning, she grabs her designer purse.
She and her bad kids rush off to church.

No structure in her personal life,
She's not equipped to be a wife.
Twenty-something with four to five kids,
Her priority is manicured nails and multiple wigs.

Sally's a sorority member,
Very elegant at Christmas dinner.
Ivy League–educated, a mind intellectually keen,
Emotional damage with low self-esteem.
Hangin' in the club is part of her gig.
Don't complain about her fatherless kids.
Got the nerve to demand respect,
Doggin' the mailman about her welfare check,
Will put an invisible rope around your neck.
Son, you don't need a girl like Sally.
She's not the type you should marry.
Mother of the earth, she's become a disgrace,
Self-seeking and outta place.
The comfort of a wife is a deeply hidden treasure,
It exceeds looks or sexual pleasure.

Oh yeah, she's cute, a real good charmer,
Searching for weakness in your emotional armor.
Her life is filled with hidden drama,
Educated by her hurt, abused mama.
You may see Sally on the Maury show,
Searching for her baby's daddy 'cause she doesn't know.

Black Girls Rock

It doesn't matter what circle you're in,
Being honest with yourself allows freedom to begin.
Masquerading in titles, degrees, and styles, hiding behind seductive
fake smiles, shopping for companionship with each glance
There's nothing profitable in a one-night romance.

The world as you view it is coming to a close,
Hidden hurt and motives to be exposed.
In her eyes sits shame and guilt, emotions dressed in an imaginary quilt.
Single mom's the name of the game
Little brothers and sisters with different names.
Competing for a man's attention,
Her job is the first thing mentioned.
Will this be another one-night stand?
A ratio of seven women to one man.
Black love in a disastrous condition,
A shortage of men with much competition.
Seventy percent of Black males in jail,
Our community is a living hell.
Blindly navigating the relationship's course
Consistently making the wrong choice,
Living for the weekend again and again.
How did it start, and when will it end?

Man-Child

Rarely he smiles, man-child running wild.
Another victim in the crowd.
A dim light once shined so bright, seeking peace in a spiritual fight.
Opportunities stumbled over, never taken.
A life of denial, continuous faking.
Groping in darkness, he goes about.
Practical thinking has been kicked out.
What happened to the youthful years?
Sixty-something in captivity to fears.
Ambition and dreams disappeared.
Unable to manage his anger,
Responsibility a definite stranger.
Abused as a child, man-child running wild,
Struggling with drugs and an alternative lifestyle.

The Living Dead

Seeking a promotion minus knowledge or devotion,
Give the boss a chance at a glance in her spandex pants;
Some off-the-clock romance, a few hours' lap dance.
Scrambling for riches and fame;
A house full of babies with different names.
Consumed with thirst for power, she has no shame.
Nine months this seed you carry;
Forty-eight percent of Black females never marry.

Too blind to see the bigger vision, women over men create greater
    division.
Fruit never falls far from the tree; my children are a reflection of me.
Seducing the boss to get in his face,
Competing with other sisters, she has no disgrace.
God's chosen people to the nations,
Living in sin, ignorance, and humiliation;
Unfathered children from generation to generation.
The good reverend preached Li'l Pookie's in a better place;
His record says he was a criminal, a killer of his race.
This game is systematically rehearsed.
Adam didn't check Eve, and the roles were reversed.
For true knowledge, we have no thirst.
This spandex generation is alive and well,
Morality and integrity up for sale.

Braggin', boastin' you're a queen,
Living a credit-card lifestyle—a pipe dream;
Inwardly suffering low self-esteem.
Hustlin' everybody you meet;
Creeping with your neighbor's husband down the street.
Welfare LaQuisha has multiple names,
From state to state, working her welfare game.
Violating the laws of the land;
In church every Sunday but not honoring God's commands.
God's *law* ain't going anywhere;
Her children living a vision of hopelessness and despair.

Damaged Goods

Black love is in a disastrous condition,
A shortage of responsible men, much competition.
Seventy percent of Black males saturate our jail,
The stench of death an ongoing smell.
Fatherless daughters with no direction,
Victims of abuse, seeking love and protection.
From eternity's throne, the Almighty cries,
He sanctioned marriage, be fruitful and multiply.
Less than twenty-five years on the planet,
Starving for a father's love, easy access is granted.

Dead Men Walking

Allow me to show you how rebellion looks.
She was the first piece of candy you took.
Truth was there, waiting to unfold.
Rebellion was the lie you told; she became married to your soul.
Rebellion became a close friend, escorted you off to state pen.

She evicted innocence, and now you're bound;
Her shackles of oppression weigh you down.
When Mama told you, "Clean your room and make your bed,"
You slipped out to play instead.

Drive-bys you commit without guilt,
Rebellion is the criminal record you built.
No remorse when you commit a murder,
Perverted lifestyle undercover.

Rebellion was violating the teacher's authority,
Mugshots flashed on prime-time TV.

Falling Apart

You've marched, sat in, rioted, and demonstrated,
Yet you remain unemancipated.
Maybe we should've remained segregated.
Not to learn the ways of the stranger,
Now our lives are in eternal danger?
Our sinful ways continue to expand,
A loss of identity in a foreign land.
A sign, a wonder, a byword among nations,
The apple of God's eye, Prince over his creation.
Entangled with madness, poverty, and shame,
Always seeking others to blame.
Living in darkness, you can't see,
Keeping the law grants liberty.
Racism's a card played by men;
It was dealt the day Adam sinned.
Carnal lifestyle, works of the flesh,
It's sin that's creating your stress,
Will you ever confess?
Anger management—a terrible joke;
Tyshawn's fingers griped around Sh'quita's throat.

Emasculation 101

Strong Black females make Black males weak,
Seeking a place to eat and sleep,
Never responsible to stand on his own feet.
Whose name's on the rent receipt?
This video on constant repeat.
Rarely does he have his own spot;
Mama or his woman calls the shots.
Seeking any female to have his back;
Unemployment check spent on crack.
A sharp tongue cuts like a knife;
Her weapon to destroy and emasculate a brother's life.
The stage opened with Mama;
"Who's my daddy, Mama?" drama.

Black Boys, Your Mothers Are Praying for You

O young Black boys, the spirit of rebellion desires to destroy
Disobedience will kill you, boy
From the ark of love, Mama's warm embrace
Her prayers to Jesus, your hiding place
Down dark city streets and bloody alleyways, rebellion's seducing
    sons to go astray
To abort an inheritance Jesus gave to you
A royal priesthood laid up for you
You are of a chosen few; build and accomplish, that's what you do.

Forces you've yet to comprehend want to bring you to a violent end
Blinded by ignorance to how it's done, Black boys on both ends of
    the gun
Crowded prison houses, locked away, fighting for your life like Sugar
    Ray.
O young Black boys, your mothers are praying for you
On the news almost every day, why did my son die this way?

Black boys, your mothers are weeping for you
You hear it in the media, you witness violence every day
The price for fame when rebellion has her way
The wages of sin is always death, let the God of Israel order our steps.

Surely, you shall not see the master's face
You've rejected his mercy, spat on his grace
You'll spend eternity in the lake of fire
You ran from the truth and pursued the liar.

Black boy, the devil's plan is to sift you as wheat
He deceived you to believe fame and fortune are ever so sweet
The lust of the eyes, the silver and the gold has you outta control.

He's given you the cars, money, and gold
A small token in exchange for your soul
The honeys and your homies watching you rise to the top
It's time to cry out to Christ or end up like Tupac.

Satan comes to steal, kill, and destroy
You're at the top of his list, Black boy
So you dream of a Bentley, a mansion on a hill
But in the end, you're bound to his will
Hey, young brother, we all shall reap what we sow
Penitentiary or death row.

I know the one who can pull you out
Have faith in Jesus and give him a shout
Have you ever wondered why Satan opposes you so?
Without the truth of the Holy Bible, you shall never know.

Black boys, your mothers are weeping for you
They know the forces of hell that are destroying you
To keep you bound, uneducated, and locked in
Satan tells you that you will never be equal to other men
His intent is to keep you in a rut
In the God of Abraham you must trust
To pull you from an impoverished life to rule and reign with Jesus
     Christ.

For far too long, you've dwelled on past mistakes
You've built a fortress of bitterness and hate
You're fighting an enemy you've never known
This battle is spiritual, not flesh and bones
Guard the words that proceed from your jaw
Fear God and keep his law
Meditate on the challenges you're going through
The next drive-by victim may be you.

Slick Willie Way's Games

What you put out is what you get back.
Cautious of every move, you can't relax.
Slippin' out on lunch,
You and your homies smokin' blunts.

Now you falsify documents and lie,
Confronted with truth you can't deny.
Makin' excuses for self-destructive ways,
No thought of consequences—mind in a daze.
Childish games being slick, immaturity, emotionally sick.
Out talkin' everybody, making no sense at all,
Here comes the pink slip, your final call.
Peepin' when you have the chance,
Stealing from the job to change your circumstance.

Time Bomb

Never was I taught discipline, nor respect.
What does this system expect?
Didn't think my attitude would lead to killin';
To survive, I started drug dealin',
Filled with rage trapped inside,
Being overlooked, cast aside.
Don't talk about the Bible or religion;
Fondled by the good reverend while fishin'.
Sometimes I wanna die; real gangstas don't cry.
Economically assassinated, socially not appreciated,
A conglomerate of hopes and dreams obliterated!

A Father's Prayer for His Sons

Father direct my sons, wherever they go,
Lord Jesus become their hero.
Cause them to meditate on Bible verses,
May they keep your laws and remember the curses.
They are tender branches abiding in the vine.
Grant them wisdom to utilize their time.
Lord, keep them from drugs and crime.
May critical thinking guide their feet.
Preserve them from the vicious streets.
Not overtaken by temptation if they became weak,
Handcuffed in a cop's back seat.
Allow your Holy Spirit to impact their decision,
Not infected by poison on television.
May they remain conscious of the tools that touch their hands,
Never committing violence against their fellow man.

Hidden Treasures

Eve, mother of all upon the earth,
Her rebellion caused this terrible curse.
Butt shakers, unwed baby makers,
Unlearned mothers, family violators.
When sin entered, perfection was reversed.
Ebony was the color of the first woman on earth.
Rebellion orchestrated this fall from such a high estate,
The mother of the human race.

False eyelashes, fake fingernails,
Colored wigs, and weaves Asians sell,
Very popular for switching her tail.
Imitating Britney Spears and Marilyn Monroe,
Her true identity, she doesn't know.
Your black skin is a delight to me;
Folks pay thousands for a tan you got free.

The rhythm in your walk,
It can't be duplicated; it can't be bought.

So soar, my sisters, above how this world makes you feel.
The essence of womanhood is the real deal,
God's divine choice of feminine appeal.
Your status, the carnal minded can't measure.
Shine out of the world's darkness,
My hidden treasure.

Sweet Memories

When I'd come home from school after a fight,
You'd shower me with a hug, and everything was all right.
The smell of hot fried chicken and biscuits filled my head.
Family stories you told before we went to bed.
Our neighborhood was flooded with despair, racism, and pain.
Mama, you gave me faith to always trust God for change.
Remembering how you got up each day to go to work for us,
Your body aching as you walked to catch the bus.
You endured much to make a decent life for my brothers, my sisters,
    and me,
Like a strong branch that never falls from the tree.
Watching from the kitchen window, your kids jump rope in the play-
    ground down below,
Motown sounds on the AM radio.
In the summer, we kids had it made, popsicles and plenty of Kool-Aid.
As I observe the world today, mothers aren't made the old-school way.
Children void of love and direction,
Mothers without natural affection,
Immeasurable love, tears of joy, and a warm smile.
I am blessed simply because I am your child

My Chocolate Candy

Oh how it warms my heart so
As I gaze upon your motherly glow.
You are appreciated more than you know,
The unconditional love you sow.
I drink from your wisdom, a fountain of life.
More valuable than precious gems, it has no price.
The strength of God radiates from within,
Nourishment to my soul, I rise again.
Seeds of love and kindness, you plant into others,
I'm grateful to God you're my children's mother.

Family Drama

Tick, tock, tick, tock, twenty-four, twenty-four around the clock.
Innocent victims being shot, reality is it won't stop.
The same elephant in the room,
Lives filled with gloom and doom.
How did this madness start? Who's buying body parts?
The same scene in every state, uncontrollable murder rate,
Even the babies can't escape.

Rebellion's door is open wide, God's Word tossed aside.
Unfathered children in rule, shoot-outs in *our* schools.
Watching violent video games, seeds planted in our children's brain.
Babies makin' babies one after another,
Rising up to kill their brother, Mama's got another lover.

Daddy busted her, then left home,
Gossiping with friends on her cell phone.
Daddy caught the n——, he pulled the trigger,
Sentenced to twenty years up the river.

Check Yo'self

Convinced you got a li'l class,
You went from a beer bottle to a champagne glass,
So you meditate on your past; time passes really fast.
In life we have a choice, a hood mentality twisting your voice
Circumstances make some think; your attitude truly stinks
Your behavior caused a lot of drive-by shootings
Your ignorant mouth keeps on polluting.

In a constant battle with depression.
Outta order, this female aggression.
Breathing contention and strife.
Do you qualify to be a wife?
Living a miserable life,
Brainwashed by this world's education,
You've made a Satanic motivated proclamation;
Your mission is global domination
Obsessed with being in control, your son's confused about his role.

Females in charge of the new paradigm,
Committing a natural and spiritual crime;
Everywhere you turn, females calling shots,
Atmosphere intense and very hot.
Yo' baby's daddy home's a prison cell
An outta-control train that derailed
He, too, raised by an unmarried female
Seeking to be loved and protected
In Big Mama's womb, you were rejected.

Friday night fight every week, handcuffed in the cop's back seat
Hopes of Ray Quan making the NBA
Success has finally come the family's way
Too much money for Quan to handle
Indicted in a national drug scandal
Rolex watches, designer gym shoes
Paying off attorneys while singing the blues
Meditating on the mistakes you've made
Peddling dope in your dressed up Escalade
In the blink of an eye, it all can fade.

Transformation

Upon my release from jail,
I can't go back to this livin' hell.
My soul's in bondage to that familiar smell,
Pushin' drugs I can no longer sell.
Life's a gamble, like rollin' dice.
Maybe I'll check out the story of Christ.
As I meditate, I've got nothing to lose.
It's time for a new dance, stop living the blues,
Build some structure, obey the rules.
Seems my life is one big curse.
I heard this is a Bible verse.
Now is the time to get my life in order,
A wild animal in the express lane to slaughter.
In survival mode, I've lived,
Always taking, never taught to give.
The spirit of death shadows me.
In constant torment, my soul's starvin' to be free.

Blindsided

Israel, O Israel, stop seeking acceptance and promotion.
Serving Babylon has become your devotion.
Lusting after power saturates your heart.
Your fragmented soul's falling apart.

A nation of priests, prophets, and kings.
Materialism, worldly fame, you dream.
Rebellion's fingers grip your neck.
Blaming others for a lack of respect.
Protesting, marching won't change your situation.
Your deliverance starts in Genesis and ends in the book of Revelation.
Truth grants options to resist all temptation.

Thoughts

Some thoughts, when realized,
Compel one to apologize.
Thoughts introduced me to this curse,
The first snatching of an old lady's purse.
Reflecting on thoughts allowed in,
A history of rebellion equals sin.

The road traveled is bumpy, not smooth,
Being slick, skippin' school,
Violating everybody's rules.
My environment, those like me,
Standing before a judge, making a plea,
A verdict of murder lurking over me.

Thoughts have the ability to make one excel;
Do not allow bitterness, envy, or anger to swell.
Meditate on living, doing good,
As God commands we all should.
As a man thinks, so is he;
Positive thoughts create liberty.

Living on the Edge

Hiding her past with many an excuse,
Soul suffering emotional and sexual abuse.
Thinking she's crazy,
Fantasizing, and just lazy.

Housekeeping ain't her thing,
She dreams of a wedding ring,
Life flooded in mystery and drama,
A missing dad, stressed-out mama.

Sometimes she dresses like a boy,
Soul tormented, empty of joy.
Truth is in the eyes; the eyes don't lie.
Temporary solace, so she stays high.
Thoughts scrambled and twisted inside
As she contemplates suicide.

Confessions

Father God, forgive me for my carnal ways,
The illegitimate children I went out and made,
My babies' mamas got the child support system lookin' for me.
She didn't know I feared responsibility.
The fruit never falls far from the tree;
My daddy abandoned Mama and me.

Lord, forgive me for not diligently seekin' you,
Studying your Word, and receiving instructions from you,
Chasin' after the world and material gain,
All my possessions must be designer-named
Got plenty of money, ridin' Mercedes Benz,
In the back seat, with the wife of my preacher friend.

Controlled by my flesh, enslaved to sin,
In fellowship with insecure, hurting, Christian men.
I must confess I am not content with my life.
Am I the reason I can't keep a wife?

O Lord, hear my plea: deliver me from homosexuality.
Deliver the church leader who molested me.
Come, O Lord, and father me; mold me into the man I desire to
Be to overcome the fears that control me.

Forgive me for the murders I committed and the law doesn't
Know, as I spend time on death row, reaping the seed I sow.
Deliver me from hurtful things that were said,
Big-lip nigger with the nappy head, kid's makin' jokes 'bout my
Jailbird dad

People never gave positive attention to me.
Now, I must prove myself in ministry!

Fear Factors

Avoiding responsibility, motives of the heart,
Truth reveals what's in the dark.
Truth is never some lucky charm.
It's like the first hit of crack in the arm.
Truth undresses the fears of one's soul.
Truth loosens the shackles, granting you control.
At God's appointed time, truth arrives at your door,
Through generations you attempted to ignore.
For temporary comfort, you hide out on dope,
Hustling Mama for money to help you cope.
When a woman sees behind your veil,
You create excuses, then hit the trail

Naked City Blues

From the East to the West Coast,
Blacks killing Blacks about who's the GOAT.
None of this makes any sense,
Yo' life stays on defense.
Entire cities in fear and suspense,
Politicians lying and outta breath.
Community activists say it's mental health.
For stepping on somebody's shoes,
Your very life you may lose.
And everyone has an excuse.
No structure at home or in class,
Repeated offenders deserves a pass.
When was the last time you tapped Calvonte's a——?
Adults afraid of little kids,
Responsible parents off the grid,
Little girls in the thug game.
Are vaccines affecting their brains?
America's become the Wild, Wild West.
Black Lives Matter printed across yo' chest.
Rebellious to everybody's rules,
Whatever happened to prayer in school?

Tricked

You won't know who you are until you open the Holy Book.
A lost identity, so you change your look,
Bleachin' your skin to resemble Barbie and Ken,
Believin' lies you've been fed,
Ashamed of your thick lips and nappy head,
Wearing colored wigs and weaves instead.

Sold your soul for this world's goods,
Faded memories back in the hood.
Tax evasion, some time in jail,
Riding the express lane on your way to hell.
Bigger and better ain't always good,
Missing real friends from the old neighborhood.

Can't trust anybody in this Hollywood game,
Watching your back, trying to remain sane.
Suspicious of everybody, who can you trust?
Another puppet to bite the dust.
The price of fame is costly, not free,
A blood sacrifice required of thee,
Your every move magnified on TV.
Things you desire to speak, you wish you could,
Secret codes in the occult brotherhood.
Trapped in the valley of decision, you hesitate.
Call on Jesus; it's not too late.

Jealousy

Insecurity comes in various shades.
It's nothing to do with status
Nor the environment where you were made.

Jealousy's objective is to enslave one's soul,
Contaminating the mind, gaining control.
Her mission is to completely destroy,
Incarcerating your life, stealing purpose and joy.
A vault filled with big ideas and dreams,
Unlocked by deceit and multiple schemes.
Never one lost for words,
Surviving on attention over talks to be heard.
Jealousy hides in the midst of family and friends,
Coveting the character someone else is in.

Rotten Fruit

What you see is built on corruption and lies;
Those drawn to this feast are hungry, desperate flies.
A lack of identity causes multitudes to blend in,
Souls nurtured by the praises of men,
Desperate for a title next to your name,
Abusive to others, creating stress and pain,
Rewarded with materialism and fame,
No consciousness or shame,
Arrogant, filled with pride,
Morality and compassion tossed aside.
A lifestyle of images—moments of temporary joy
Showing off in your big-boy toy.
Driving too fast, you can miss the warning sign;
Rebellion has overloaded your mind.
One day, your world will come crashing;
Sin has become your greatest passion.
Like a wild deer hit while crossing the street;
Unrighteousness, a setup for destruction and defeat.

SoulSearching

A loudmouth, don't know your place,
Your men crossing over to another race,
No control over your personal life.
Are you equipped to be a wife?
Twenty-something with four or five kids,
Your priorities are manicured nails and colored wigs.
Tight jeans strutting down the avenue,
Government programs taking care of you.

Got the nerve to demand respect,
Doggin' the mailman 'bout your welfare check,
Bad attitude demanding respect,
An invisible rope around your neck.
Sister, you make life easy for those callin' the shots,
Generations spent on the same ghetto blocks.
Your son's dying in the streets,
Lost and fatherless, you made him weak.

Mother of the earth, you have become a total disgrace,
No understanding of structure and outta place.
Comfort of a man is a deep hidden treasure;
It exceeds sexual pleasure.

Never Back Away

On this journey, chasing my dream;
Adults, too, have secret schemes
Because we're young and tender;
Many have a private agenda.
Oh yeah, they were ballers back in the day
But rarely do what they say;
In your parent's pocket, they stay.
Pretending to help you in the right direction,
Never producing any positive connection,
Always with an excuse—this, too, is child abuse
Lying through his gold teeth,
Causing dad stress and grief.
Concealing anger rising in my chest,
I'm tempted to put my homies on this thief, I confess,
So I pray to the Lord and give it a rest.
Vengeance is the Lord's; he shall repay.
Focusing on my dream, in the gym, I stay.

Walking in the Spirit

Complacency, not a companion;
I'm being transformed by an unspeakable fervency.
Dominion is my portion.
Expansion echoes in my ear.
Truth and understanding, nourishment to my soul.
Transition seducing me, the pathway awaits my arrival.
Man's knowledge is delusional, dressed in theatrical garments.
I've chosen no longer to participate;
I exit this carousel ride.
Truth has become my ally, my defender.

Pulpit Pimp

The atmosphere, a beatdown and manipulation,
Getting that money with no hesitation.
Begging is the main motivation,
Never any Bible or truthful information.
Spewing out traditional lies,
The God of the Bible, young folks despise.
Ray Ray sits with Big Mama every week.
He knows a hustle from time spent in the street.
This preacher's game is stale and very weak.
Grandma's check is what this pimp seeks.
Prosperity is all he teaches, and the brother's pockets, he can't reach;
He's nothing more than a walking leech.
His new Mercedes's parked outside,
No fear of God and filled with pride,
A church filled with women being taken for a ride.

A Prophetic Message

Begin to eat the Word for breakfast, lunch, and dinner.
Into eternal life shall you enter.
Be mindful of the food you eat,
Plenty of impurities in the street;
Bad doctrine makes one weak.
My son, lend an ear to the word of life and
Present your mind—gifts as a holy sacrifice.
Remain mindful of eternal glory,
Be instant in season, ready to tell your story.
I've set you as a watchman on the wall.
Continue to trust in me, and answer the call.
Be strong in the power of God's might
As he launches you into greater heights.

Stunted Growth

Mixed emotions ride one's mind,
Moments of elation retrieved sometimes.
In a world filled with various attitudes,
In desperate need of biblical food,
Our existence formed from the dust.
In man's intellect, we put our trust.
Opinions are as grains of sand.
The Alpha and the Omega created man.
Faith and understanding work hand in hand.
We've interrupted God's perfect plan.
Surely, all is vanity, mankind goes about.
Peace is aborted when God is left out.

About the Author

John O. Gray is the president of Man in the Mirror Foundation, a nonprofit organization that mentors young men and homeless veterans. In 2017, Man in the Mirror was adopted by the Chicago Public Schools' Urban Prep Academy.

As a writer and motivational speaker, John utilizes rhymes about life lessons as an essential tool to encourage young men to honestly evaluate their circumstances. He created a mentoring program for former Duke University basketball star Phil Henderson.

John attended Prairie State College in Chicago Heights, Illinois, to study mental health counseling. He is happily married to his best friend, Saundra, for thirty years. His mentoring program began with his three sons, who are all college graduates and have matured into well-disciplined, successful men.